The Cambridge Five: The History and Lega
Ring in Britain during World War II and the Cold War

By Charles River Editors

Kim Philby, one of the members

About Charles River Editors

Charles River Editors is a boutique digital publishing company, specializing in bringing history back to life with educational and engaging books on a wide range of topics. Keep up to date with our new and free offerings with this 5 second sign up on our weekly mailing list, and visit Our Kindle Author Page to see other recently published Kindle titles.

We make these books for you and always want to know our readers' opinions, so we encourage you to leave reviews and look forward to publishing new and exciting titles each week.

Introduction

Donald Maclean, one of the members

The Cambridge Five

The spy novel emerged from the intrigues of the mid-20th century for good reason. The war with the Third Reich involved an unseen cloak and dagger struggle between the participants, but beyond that, an even larger and longer contest took place in the shadows.

Communism gained its first major foothold in statehood with the success of the Russian Revolution at the end of World War I, a success bizarrely assisted by the massive funding provided to the revolutionaries by some Western businessmen. Armand Hammer's father Julius, for instance, gave the new Soviet Union $50,000 in gold to back their new currency. In exchange he received asbestos mining and oil concessions, plus a pencil manufacturing monopoly in the USSR lasting until the Stalin era.

Soviet Russia followed a philosophy demanding international, global revolution – which, in practice, often resembled conquest by any means available, direct or indirect. While the Soviets never hesitated to use naked force when it seemed advisable, or when compelled to it by outside attack, they made intensive use of covert operations – spying, assassination, bribery, infiltration of governments and educational systems, the deployment of agents provocateur and "agitprop" – in an effort to weaken other nations from within or possibly cause takeover by a friendly revolutionary regime.

Soviet agents operated in all European countries and others, but their main efforts naturally focused on the strongest potential rivals – Germany, the United States, and Great Britain. Intelligent, persistent, and ruthless, the Soviets succeeded in recruiting a considerable number of agents, including men from the British ruling class.

Their activities enabled the Soviets to capture and execute hundreds, if not thousands, of the opponents of their regime along with numbers of British agents. The men responsible for this unprecedented leaking of life-or-death information would enter history as the Cambridge Five – though in fact, they may have been only the core of a much larger group.

The Cambridge Five: The History and Legacy of the Notorious Soviet Spy Ring in Britain during World War II and the Cold War chronicles the war's most infamous spy ring and its activities. Along with pictures of important people, places, and events, you will learn about the Cambridge Five like never before.

Soviet Agents in the West

The Soviet doctrine of recruiting long-term agents in western countries originated long before it enmeshed the Cambridge Five in its nets, emerging from the hard reality of Soviet military overreach and defeat when the "Five" were still small children, being ignored by their parents and raised by a series of nannies. The victories and defeats on far-off battlefields in Eastern Europe would have an overwhelming effect on the destiny of the men's lives, due to the strategic necessities imposed on communist expansionism.

Still engaged in the Russian Civil War in 1919, the newly minted Soviet Russia set its sights on immediate, violent expansion of the realm of Marxism and Communism in the world. The communists viewed highly industrialized and powerful Germany as a great revolutionary prize, one whose fall to Soviet domination would trigger a chain reaction of revolution over the entire globe. Even as the Russian Civil War raged, a German civil war had begun, pitting the communist Spartacist League and the Communist Party of Germany against the nationalistic Freikorps and other paramilitary fighting leagues.

The Soviets wanted to link up with their communist brethren in Germany for mutual support in bringing about a revolutionary takeover of Eastern and Central Europe as a springboard to further communist victories. However, Poland stood in the way of this vision. As Soviet Marshal Mikhail Tukhachevsky thundered in his Order of the Day on July 2nd, 1920, "To the West! Over the corpse of White Poland lies the road to world-wide conflagration. March on Vilno, Minsk, Warsaw!"

Tukhachevsky

Lenin himself expressed a desire to "probe Europe with the bayonets of the Red Army" in an effort to trigger universal revolution, and the Red Army accordingly moved against Poland. The Soviets, however, had not considered two forces – Polish nationalistic patriotism, which motivated even the humblest Pole to meet the invader with force despite the communists' claims of acting as liberators, and Marshal Jozef Pilsudski. Over the course of slightly more than two years and one month, the Soviets and Poles mauled one another in a chaotic struggle. Though often carried on in an amateurish fashion, the Polish-Soviet War reaped a bloody harvest on both sides, leading to more than 100,000 total deaths. In the end, the Soviets failed to either conquer the Poles by force of arms or to trigger a communist revolution in the country. A patriotic survival instinct moved Poles of all classes to side primarily with men of their own nation, baffling Lenin's hopes of exterminating the "kulaks" and landowners on the way to the borders of Germany, the real prize desired by the communists.

Pilsudski

Lenin, of course, interpreted this love of country and loyalty to their ethnic and cultural group as a combination of stupidity and malice on the part of the Poles: "The Poles thought, and acted, not in a social, revolutionary way but as nationalists, as imperialists. The revolution in Poland which we counted on, did not take place. The workers and peasants, deceived by Pilsudski and Daszynski, defended their class enemy and let our brave Red soldiers starve, ambushed them, and beat them to death. [...] We had to make peace." (Davies, 2003, 266). The communist who recorded this speech by Lenin went so far as to describe Lenin's facial expression at the suffering of the workers as resembling that of Grunewald's depiction of Jesus Christ and called the Bolshevik leader a "man of sorrows."

Lenin

Regardless of whatever burdens the "folly" of the indomitable Poles put on Lenin's shoulders, the defeat prompted a sharp change in the methods of Soviet imperialism. Rather than hoping to win immediately by force of arms, the Soviets switched to a strategy of ruthless, persistent subversion in the western nations. As part of this program, they set about recruiting as many sleeper agents as possible in Germany, France, England, America, and other nations, as well as providing backing and advice to many local revolutionary movements. Only the late 1930s and early 1940s would military expansionism begin to reappear as a major Soviet strategy in Europe.

Born in 1903 in Czechoslovakia, a man named Arnold Deutsch would prove critical to spreading Soviet recruitment to Britain and bringing the Cambridge Five into the Soviet fold. The scion of a Jewish family, Deutsch possessed a link to England long before he actually traveled there thanks to his cousin Oscar Deutsch, a successful capitalist. A branch of the Deutsch family moved to Britain in the 19th century, amassing a fortune selling scrap metal, and Oscar Deutsch used that money to start the "Odeon" cinema chain. The name derived from the word for an ancient Greek amphitheater used for dramatic performances, but Oscar Deutsch, striking on a catchy advertising gimmick, soon claimed it represented an acronym for "Oscar Deutsch Entertains Our Nation."

Arnold Deutsch studied chemistry in Vienna, earning a doctorate at the age of 24 in 1927. More significantly for history, he joined the Communist Party while at school, becoming an ardent revolutionary Marxist. The woman he married in 1929, Josefine, also belonged to the communist party. "Fini," as he called her familiarly, secretly worked as an agent of the Comintern, or the Communist International, an organization headquartered in Moscow and dedicated to worldwide revolution, peaceful or violent as necessary.

Deutsch also involved himself in the "Sex-Pol" or "Sexual Politics" movement of Wilhelm Reich, a sexually obsessed communist who styled himself a "sexologist" and attempted to recruit new communists through his study and explanation of "better orgasms." Deutsch, also sexually insatiable, linked himself avidly to Sex-Pol, almost coming to grief as a consequence. The Viennese antipornography police hunted for him on the eve of his departure for England thanks to his incautious promotion of Reich's work.

Josefine Deutsch, operating under the alias of Liza Kramer, served as a covert radio operator for Viennese revolutionaries. She provided go-between communications services for the communists in Vienna and their Comintern masters in Moscow. She also gave her husband an introduction to the central organization itself, the couple journeying to Moscow in January 1932 so that Arnold could become a vetted and bona fide agent of the International Department of the Comintern. He also joined the NKVD in August 1932, receiving thorough training as a spy, spymaster, and agent provocateur.

Deutsch left Vienna soon after his return from the Soviet Union and traveled to London, using his actual name. This enabled him to show off his admittedly impressive academic credentials to win admission to London University as a "researcher" – a vague post which gave him freedom to move about the university and the country without being tied to an employer or schedule.

He almost immediately started hosting lavish dinners, winning many friends through his outgoing, cheerful personality. Nobody wondered how an obscure researcher from Vienna could live in such constantly high style. In fact, a steady supply of NKVD funds arrived in Deutsch's bank account so that he could establish himself as a notable person – one well placed to recruit large numbers of important agents for Comintern.

Fatefully, Deutsch met a university friend, another fanatical communist and revolutionary named Edith Suschitzky, now living in London with her British husband under the name of Edith Tudor-Hart. Alexander Tudor-Hart, a descendant of the wealthy New York businessman Ephraim Hirz (who changed his name to Hart after moving to America), nevertheless professed revolutionary communism himself. He would later serve as a volunteer medic for the communist Republicans during the Spanish Civil War.

Meanwhile, Edith Tudor-Hart worked in Vienna as a photographer, using her photography for communist commentary and propaganda, while also secretly working with revolutionaries seeking to win Austria for communism. The abortive 1933 revolution, during which the Austrian nationalist Dollfuss government decisively crushed the Red revolutionaries, forced the Tudor-

Harts to flee back to London or risk being shot.

Arnold Deutsch and Edith Tudor-Hart met in London, though who initiated the contact remains lost to history. Deutsch officially recruited Tudor-Hart as a Comintern agent, providing the NKVD, the notorious People's Commissariat of Internal Affairs for the Soviet Union (which by this time had taken over the functions of the Cheka and other secret police groups), with his written recommendation: "I knew her from Vienna in 1926. She is about thirty. She married an English doctor and in May came to Britain. She works as a photographer and has a studio. She is one of the most celebrated children's photographers in England. I met her soon after her arrival in Britain. She immediately agreed to work for us." (Costello, 1993, 134).

Edith Tudor-Hart served as a sort of "talent scout" for Deutsch, socializing with many people (a task made easy by the fame of her photography studio) and then arranging for those who expressed communist sympathies and seemed likely to offer something as agent to meet with Deutsch himself. Fatefully, in June 1934, she set up a meeting between Deutsch and a young upper-class Britisher named Harold "Kim" Philby, the first member of the infamous "Cambridge Five."

Recruiting the Cambridge Five

All of the men who would become the "Cambridge Five" came from the British upper class, with an affluent background and a good education. Such men formed the backbone of Britain's various intelligence services, including the famous MI6. In order to join the intelligence service, in fact, all a young Englishman needed to do was pass through the distinguished schools – Cambridge and Eton – and then contact the intelligence offices to volunteer his services. More often than not, he would be accepted on the strength of his background alone.

A certain logic informed this method of choosing intelligence agents by the British government. Not merely a technique of providing sinecures to rich young men, the system represented a genuine attempt to recruit people loyal to England and its empire.

The leadership's reasoning posited that such privileged young men held an immense stake in preserving the nation which gave them power, money, and influence. In effect, England belonged indirectly to them and, the reasoning went, people do not generally destroy their own belongings pointlessly. The youthful recruits had everything to gain by helping to preserve their nation, and everything to lose by betraying it.

While intending to provide strong bonds of fealty to the mother country, the system proved too one-dimensional and reductionist in its view of human motivation. It posited that material benefit alone would produce total loyalty, while at the same time promoting a form of child-rearing that tended to create people thirsty for actual belonging and filled with resentment and even hatred towards established, familiar authority.

British upper class fathers, following a belief of their time that this would build character, treated their sons with a mixture of coldness and contempt. Rather than paying attention to the next generation of the ruling class, giving them advice, and building a sense of connection with their familial and national roots by acting as friends and mentors, the older Englishmen ignored their sons except to occasionally mock them, offering pure negativity without even the saving touch of actually constructive criticism.

As a result, rather than becoming stronger, the young men produced by the English public school system grew up alienated, cut off from any sense of family continuity or affection, and desperate for camaraderie, personal affirmation, and a sense of belonging from any available source. Such men represented superb targets for recruitment by a collectivist philosophy which offered a sort of substitute family in the form of the commune and state.

The conditions of England's prep schools added another potentially destabilizing element to the emotional and mental makeup of their pupils. In addition to cutting family contact to a minimum, thus further weakening strongest bond of loyalty to family and thus to nation (which is, after all, simply an extremely extended family), the schools treated the boys as prisoners and abused them as such.

In addition to vicious floggings – typically drawing blood – for the slightest offenses, the personnel treated the boys with arbitrary sadism. The headmaster of Durnford prep school achieved notoriety by giving the heads of small boys terrific, almost stunning blows, while terrorizing them with shouted threats – not as a response for anything that they had done, but simply as an "introduction" to being in his charge. His wife forced boys to kneel on all fours so she could use them as living footstools for her bare feet while reading.

In a weirdly sadomasochistic touch, achieving good academic grades gave a student the "reward" of being allowed to flog the buttocks of lesser achievers with canes or birches when they broke the numerous petty rules. Homosexuality also proved rife among the student body, with over 20% of students willing to admit to having sex with the other boys, despite homosexuality's illegality at the time. A system which fostered homosexual relations (however accidentally) while simultaneously making those relations a career-ruining or even criminal offense naturally provided a target-rich environment for unscrupulous foreign blackmailers.

Despite the fact many men retained loyalty to England despite such mistreatment, just about all of them emerged from the early 20th century prep school system with a deep loathing for authority and unwillingness to follow orders ingrained into them by the experience. Rather than building respect, the incessant petty tyrannies of the prep school officials inculcated bitter resentment in many of the students – resentment which, in some cases, likely contributed to transformation into a revolutionary agent. The British establishment created a system in which it gave its rising young stars, charged with defending the Empire, complete financial fulfillment, while denying them any real sense of belonging or emotional fulfillment. It expected this to produce absolute loyalty, overlooking the fact that the complex human mind requires more than one type of coin to secure its loyalty. The Soviets would at least pretend to address those other needs, and as a result recruited some of Cambridge's "best and brightest."

Once released from this prolonged and profoundly alienating treatment, the boys – now young men – usually went on to higher education at Eton and Cambridge, learned the social graces and reasoning skills that would make many of the Cambridge Five suave, charming, and persuasive. These traits, while very useful to a genuine public servant, also provided an ideal mask for a man selling out his nation to a hostile foreign power.

One of the most notorious of the spies, Harold "Kim" Philby, arrived in Cambridge at age 17. He was the son of St. John Philby, a man full of hubris who took British upper class neglect of his offspring to the extreme. The elder Philby completely ignored both his offspring and his wife, spending most of the time away pursuing his social climbing or engaged in ornithology. Philby's mother also paid him scant heed despite her own loneliness, and a Punjabi nanny raised the young Kim during his early years.

Nominally studying history, Kim Philby met two of the other "Cambridge Five" almost upon his arrival – Donald Maclean, a linguist, and Guy Burgess, a man with razor-sharp wit, a formidable if chaotic intellect, and fanatical devotion to communist principles. Philby, interestingly, went through the motions of becoming a communist, but apparently never bothered to study it.

He joined the Socialist Society and bought a set of Karl Marx's works which then remained unread on his shelf, but showed no sign that he ever attempted to understand communist theory beyond an utterly superficial "Robin Hood" image of heroic communists standing up against the oppressors of the poor. The communists of his Cambridge Five clique and the Comintern agents he dealt with had become his substitute family, and with that emotional emptiness filled, there remained no need for deeper cerebration.

British complacency and indifference to the risks of communist agents stand out starkly in Philby's recruitment to Soviet service. At around the time of his graduation in 1933, Philby simply walked to the office of a known Marxist economics professor, Maurice Dobb, and asked him point-blank how he could join the communist cause. Dobb, with equally fearless candor, sent him directly to Louis Giberti, a Comintern recruitment agent in Paris.

Upon his arrival in Paris, Philby met with Giberti, who sent him on to Vienna. The Englishman arrived at precisely the moment that the conflict between communist revolutionaries and the nationalist government under Engelbert Dollfuss came to a head. Philby's communist contacts in Austria, Israel Kohlmann and his wife Gisella, had a daughter, Alice or "Litzi," who in turn had dedicated herself to revolution and had direct links to Soviet intelligence. Litzi and Philby soon began a passionate sexual relationship which utterly enthralled the previously virginal Philby. He joined her in the brief Austrian civil war, which saw the communists and labor forces utterly crushed and their leaders shot. The couple married on February 24th, 1934, which effectively gave Litzi an escape route, since Philby's British citizenship gave him hermetic protection against the Austrian police, who had no wish to trigger a diplomatic incident by detaining a foreigner, even an openly communist one.

Philby's mother worried about his communist connections when he returned home, but his father – then chasing advancement and birds in Saudi Arabia – shrugged the matter off as a passing phase. As it turned out, Philby's mother proved correct in her anxiety.

On top of all this, Edith Tudor-Hart and Litzi Kohlmann had known one another in the small world of Viennese revolutionary life. In May 1934, Edith invited Litzi and her husband over to tea with her and her husband. There, the four communists shared their experiences of the conflict in Vienna while sipping tea in thoroughly British fashion. Edith Tudor-Hart took note of Philby's evident communist zeal as well as his English upper-class suavity and sang froid, and immediately decided he would make a superb Soviet agent. She informed Deutsch of her find and together they badgered their cautious Comintern superiors into allowing them a highly accelerated recruitment of the young Englishman. Sometime in early June, Tudor-Hart brought Philby to meet with Deutsch, then operating under the code-name Otto.

Using every trick she knew, Tudor-Hart took a series of taxis all over London, rapidly switching from one to another to shake off any potential "tail." The bemused Philby cooperated with these extravagant security procedures and eventually found himself seated on a sunny bench in Regent's Park.

Deutsch approached Philby and engaged him in conversation, talking about cultural matters and his own preference for Paris. Philby immediately formed an almost worshipful feeling of friendliness for the slightly older Deutsch: "He was a marvelous man. Simply marvelous. I felt that immediately. The first thing I noticed about him were his eyes. He looked at you as if nothing more important in life than you and talking to you existed in that moment." (MacIntyre, 2015, 40). Deutsch, of course, used his NKVD training to project just such a charismatic yet friendly demeanor. He also appraised Philby coolly and professionally, as a potential asset, possibly useful in attaining the objective of world revolution. Philby, naively enthusiastic, took Deutsch's outward persona at face value and thus swiftly fell under emotional thrall to the communists, effectively assessing them as a warm, welcoming family rather than the reality of hard, power-driven men who viewed him as an ambulatory tool.

During the first meeting, the two men spoke only obliquely of their shared purpose, assessing how much they could safely reveal to the other. Philby's earnestness shone through and Deutsch left the discussion convinced that the young Englishman possessed full dedication to the communist cause. Nevertheless, he proceeded with the care and caution of a professional, easing Philby into the world of treason and espionage while simultaneously testing his reliability.

Deutsch assigned Philby the alias "Synok," an affectionate diminutive in Russian translating approximately as "little son." This led to the parallel aliases "Söhnchen" in German and "Sonny" in English. While Deutsch remained clear-eyed in his analysis to a large degree, his report to the NKVD reveals that he himself may have been manipulated by Philby's plausibility and charm: "Söhnchen comes from a peculiar family. His father is considered at present to be the most distinguished expert on the Arab world…. He is an ambitious tyrant and wanted to make a great man out of his son. […] It's amazing that a young man is so widely and deeply knowledgeable… He is so serious that he forgets he is only 25." (MacIntyre, 2015, 44).

Initially, Deutsch assigned Philby three tasks: finding a career that would give him access to useful information and contacts, with Deutsch suggesting journalism; preparing a list of friends and acquaintances likely to be suitable targets for recruitment; and photographing his father's papers, especially any which looked important. While the third assignment served as a test of Philby's commitment, his communist handlers also constantly overestimated the father's importance, deeming him a top agent with crucial information about the British Empire's spy network.

Kim unhesitatingly spied on his father, taking photographs of every document he could find and passing them along to Deutsch. He also gained a lower-level editorial post at the *World Review of Reviews* and pretended to become right-wing and sympathetic to the Nazis, going so far as to join the Anglo-German Fellowship in 1935. Philby also gave a list of potential recruits to the Soviets. He drew from his many communist contacts at the universities to create this document, including two of momentous significance among the others – Guy Burgess and Donald Maclean. These would enter history as two more the Cambridge Five.

Guy Burgess sprang from well-to-do middle class stock descended from Huguenots who fled to England in 1592. A bizarre figure, born troublemaker, and graduate of Eton and Cambridge, Burgess manifested garish, melodramatic homosexuality from his university days onward, bragging constantly of outlandish sexual exploits – dancing around a table with other homosexuals in Paris while using leather whips to flog a naked boy tied onto the tabletop, involving himself in Turkish same-sex orgies, and like claims.

At one point in his later career in British intelligence, Sir Robert Mackenzie, a security officer responsible for keeping Burgess and other agents safe while abroad in the USA, received word that Burgess might involve himself in even worse scandals. Mackenzie memorable responded, "What does he mean 'worse?' Goats?"

Burgess manifested many other eccentricities. He could be extremely amusing, witty, and charming when he wished to be, while at other times he took a positive delight in taunting and provoking others into a fury, laughing at the results even if physically attacked in response. A slight but noxious odor hung around Burgess, resulting from his questionable personal hygiene. His clothes, while often expensive, appeared crumpled and dirty. He also avidly indulged in constant drinking, punctuating his usual tippling with alcoholic binges of self-destructive proportions.

Burgess' homosexuality represented an asset in the eyes of Soviets. While the NKVD preferred to avoid blackmail wherever possible when recruiting long-term spies because it led to resentment – a feeling of friendliness and comradeship being considered (and proven) to be a much better tool for manipulating people into doing the Soviets' bidding – the illegality of homosexuality left it as a latent threat behind all dealings with the spies' foreign masters. Britain's homosexuals also formed a separate clique within society, very loyal to each other but less attached to England as a whole; recruiting one, such as Burgess, often provided easy leverage to recruiting most of his homosexual friends.

Burgess got wind of Philby's new, mysterious connections and made himself as obnoxious as possible about them. According to Philby himself, he and Deutsch decided to recruit Burgess as an agent simply so that his incessant, brazenly incautious attempts to discover Philby's secret did not draw official scrutiny: "He convinced himself that Maclean and I had not undergone a sudden change of views, and that he was being excluded from something esoteric and exciting. So he started to badger us, and no one could badger more effectively than Burgess. He went for Maclean and he went for me […] He might well be more dangerous outside than inside. […] He must have been one of the very few people to have forced themselves into the Soviet special service." (Lownie, 2015, 54-55).

Deutsch recruited Donald Maclean first, then Burgess. The Soviets objected at first, wanting men not known to one another rather than close friends in order to compartmentalize their agents for greater security. However, Deutsch argued persuasively on behalf of Maclean and Burgess. The NKVD allowed their training to continue.

On July 15th, 1934, another NKVD agent arrived in England to begin running Deutsch's recruits as a serious espionage network. Many layers of deceit cloaked this man's true identity. To the authorities, based on his passport and other identifying paperwork, he appeared as a Jewish-American businessman named William Goldin, coming to England to open an import/export business. He bore the code-name Swede among the British spies he managed. Among the Soviets, he preferred to go by the name of Alexander Orlov, but at birth his parents called him Leiba "Lev" Feldbin. Orlov ran his operation from the offices of his front business, the American Refrigerator Company, located on Regent Street close to Piccadilly Circus. Provided with ample money by the Soviet government, the company operated as an actual importer of American freezers and refrigerators, providing excellent cover for covert activities. Deutsch continued to handle recruitment and training for some time, however.

Burgess supplied a list of over two hundred possible candidates for recruitment, neatly dividing the listed individuals into heterosexual and homosexual columns for the Soviets' convenience. He also worked assiduously to recruit one of his homosexual friends from Cambridge, Anthony

Blunt, who described himself as initially being no more than a "paper Marxist." Burgess persisted, finally using the start of the Spanish Civil War to badger his friend into joining Deutsch's expanding stable of communist spies.

Blunt agreed to spy for the Soviets because they proved willing to supply the communist Republican forces in Spain with troops and tanks, while the Western democracies did not. Nevertheless, this appears as a pretext, covering the actual fact that Burgess simply used his domineering personality to coerce Blunt into acting as an agent. Blunt then hid the weakness of his own character in yielding to Burgess' hectoring by seizing upon a fairly thin ideological excuse.

Blunt, though not a fanatic like Burgess or Philby, proved his worth as a man adroit at finding potential recruits and making a plausible first approach to them. Usefully, Blunt expanded the recruiting field outside the inner circles of Cambridge and Eton, successfully drawing a number of minor and major figures into the Soviet orbit.

Anthony Blunt – given the rather unsubtle initial code-name "Tony" – added several more agents to Deutsch's and Orlov's roster soon after his own 1936 recruitment. The extremely affluent American economics student Michael Straight, one of Blunt's Cambridge friends with strong communist leanings, represented his first success. Straight joined mostly due to his awestruck admiration for the worldly charm and apparent sophistication of Blunt and Burgess, by his own admission.

Much more significantly, Blunt moved on to recruit the stereotypically taciturn Scot John Cairncross. Cairncross, another Cambridge graduate, already worked for the Foreign Office – an extremely useful connection for inserting the other members of the growing spy ring into British intelligence – at the time of his 1936 recruitment by Blunt. Yuri Modin, Cairncross' postwar handler, later sketched his first impressions of the Lanarkshire native and son of an ironmongery's manager: "John Cairncross, codename the Carelian, was very much the typical Scot, with a tallish frame, bony face and darting eyes. In my experience well-bred men invariably have one or two traits which set them apart from the crowd: for example, their shoes tend to be freshly polished; their shirts may be frayed, but the collars will be stiff and starched; their trousers, even if dirty, will always have a discernible crease. Cairncross displayed not one of these telltale characteristics." (Modin, 1994, 21). Cairncross' superb mind, calm professionalism, and almost totally nondescript exterior served him well as the agent of a hostile power working against his own country.

By 1936 the Cambridge Five all worked directly for Comintern and the NKVD, and all that remained was for them to infiltrate British intelligence and carry out their mission. Thanks to England's eccentric method of vetting candidates for these extremely sensitive posts, this proved much easier than it might have in a more paranoid nation.

World War II

Both Guy Burgess and Kim Philby started their work in earnest as members of the media. Philby landed work as a correspondent for *The Times,* while with his connections, educational background, and the charm he exhibited when useful to him, Burgess got a job with the BBC. Both men enjoyed rapid professional success, building the start of apparently promising careers in the news services. These, however, represented no more than a springboard to more valuable spying positions.

Working as both a reporter and a secret communist agent allowed Philby to insert himself into the thick of the action when open conflict between communists and nationalists erupted in Spain. True to his deep cover as a right-wing sympathizer, Philby volunteered to cover the nationalist forces of Francisco Franco in the Spanish Civil War, which he did with his characteristically interesting and humorous style.

While the nationalist Spanish believed this friendly, charismatic young Englishman to be fully on their side, treating him much like a visiting celebrity journalist and even awarding him a medal for his courage in covering their struggle, they had in fact embraced a bitter enemy. Philby indeed reported on the war, but also sent copious data to his Soviet masters on Francoist troops strengths, plans, maneuvers, and even the capabilities of their vehicles and weapons. The USSR, in turn, passed this crucial military intelligence on to the communist Republican forces as quickly as possible.

Though the nationalists eventually won, it was not through lack of Philby's trying to engineer their defeat by reporting every military secret he could lay his hands on. With his charm and status as a seemingly sympathetic foreign reporter, he had no difficulty mixing with the officers and command structure of Franco's army, even at rarefied levels. He also pushed forward into danger to gain "scoops" both overt and covert. Once, the blast of a communist shell came within a hairsbreadth of killing him.

The Soviets, observing his successes and courage, soon came up with an alternate use for their spy. They sent a message to Philby's handler Theodore Maly to instruct the English agent not merely to provide intelligence, but to kill General Franco himself. This seemed a plausible enough plan to the NKVD. Philby had received the Red Cross of Military Merit from the hands of the nationalist leader himself, and also seduced the royalist Frances Doble, Lady Lindsay-Hogg, who gave him ready access to the top levels of Spanish nationalist society and leadership.

Maly found himself in a hideous predicament due to this order. The NKVD viewed any refusal to carry out an order, no matter how hare-brained and impossible, as treason and might well kill the person who refused. On the other hand, Philby would certainly die if he attempted Franco's assassination, with a very high probability of failure. Maly did not want to waste the valuable agent on probably useless suicide mission. The Hungarian screwed up his courage and rejected the order: "Even if he had been able to get close to Franco then he, despite his willingness, would not be able to do what is expected of him. For all his loyalty and willingness to sacrifice himself, he does not have the physical courage and other qualities necessary." (Borovik, 1995, 89).

The Soviets relented, though this placed dangerous suspicion on Maly. When Philby returned from Spain, he brought with him a much enhanced reputation and the air of a seasoned man of the world, who had visited foreign parts and "seen the elephant." He had also separated from Litzi in 1936, though the couple would not formally divorce until 1946. This left him free to pursue other women, a lifelong preoccupation.

At the start of World War II, *The Times* chose Philby as one of a select group of 15 correspondents who would cover the British Expeditionary Force (BEF) in France. In the meantime, Guy Burgess secured a position in England's international intelligence service, MI6.

When Philby returned from his assignment with the BEF, he found himself called in for several meetings with the chief of MI6's paramilitary operations branch, Section D (literally "Section Destruction"), Sarah Maxse. Burgess appeared at one of the later meetings, making it clear that his instrumentality brought Philby to the notice of Maxse: "[S]he turned up accompanied by Guy Burgess, whom I knew well. I was put through my paces again. Encouraged by Guy's presence, I began to show off, name-dropping shamelessly, as one does at interviews. From time to time, my interlocutors exchanged glances; Guy would nod gravely and approvingly. It turned out that I was wasting my time, since a decision had already been taken. Before we parted, Miss Maxse informed me that, if I agreed, I should sever my connection with The Times and report for duty to Guy Burgess." (Philby, 2003, 10).

The clandestine maneuverings of Deutsch and Orlov had just paid off handsomely. Valentine Vivian, a high-ranking officer in MI6, accepted the new recruit on the strength of his family origins and his "proper" education at Eton and Cambridge, with no further investigation.

Soon the leaders of British intelligence had settled the Cambridge Five into the positions they would occupy for much of the war. They soon moved Philby to Section V, while Burgess continued in the main section of MI6. Anthony Blunt worked in MI5, or domestic counter-intelligence, while John Cairncross operated at the code-breaking facility of Bletchley Park and Donald Maclean held a post at the Foreign Office, where secrets relating to communications between the Western Allied governments passed regularly through his hands.

The Cambridge Five, in short, covered the whole spectrum of different intelligence bureaus in England, from diplomacy to military intelligence to code-breaking. Their minor sub-agents extended their information gathering reach even further through the system.

At about this time, Philby met not only his mentally unbalanced future wife, Aileen Furse, who secretly cut herself and then infected the wounds with her own urine to gain sympathy and attention, but a curious mirror of himself, Nicolas Elliot. Nicolas Elliott, another important British intelligence agent, came from a background very similar to Philby's. He passed through the same schooling, had the same contempt for authority, the same persuasiveness and infectious good humor, the same taste for travel and adventure – but, utterly unlike Philby, felt unshakable loyalty to England and despised communism as a danger to the existence of European civilization itself.

Their intelligence work brought these two young men together, and friendship rapidly developed between them. Elliott had no notion of Philby's treason, and Philby seems to have genuinely liked the other man despite the hidden ideological gulf between them. Of course, this would not come between Philby and his work of furthering Soviet interests, but during the early war years, Philby and Elliott enjoyed many discussions of world affairs over lunch or with alcohol at their clubs, relaxing after long hours of sifting, digesting, and reporting intelligence to their various masters. Though neither knew it, Philby's final unmasking as a Soviet spy would also involve Nicolas Elliott.

Though they had established a remarkably successful and thorough network of spies of sleeper agents riddling MI5, MI6, and the rest of British intelligence like termites gnawing unseen in a grand old house, and they had begun recruiting large numbers of agents in America as well, the Soviet handlers of the Cambridge Five did not always prosper at the hands of the USSR. A wave of paranoia and lethal purges swept Stalinist Russia from the late 1930s and into the 1940s, and agents in foreign lands came under particular suspicion.

Many men and women found themselves recalled to the Soviet Union, where, in a large number of cases, the NKVD subsequently arrested them, forced them to admit to counterrevolutionary activity through prolonged, brutal torture, then tried and executed them on the basis of these trumped-up confessions. Such a fate befell Theodore Maly, who saved Philby from the suicide mission against General Franco. Heeding a summons to return, he worked for some time at the intelligence section in the infamous Lubyanka. However, the NKVD eventually arrested him and subjected him to torture until, to stop the pain, he signed a statement that he worked for the German Abwehr. This led to his trial and execution by firing squad.

Alexander Orlov, seeing the handwriting on the wall (and having managed to bring his wife and daughter to Britain), defected to Canada in 1938, escaping the fate that consumed many other effective Soviet agents in the West.

Arnold Deutsch also met a sticky end sometime during these years – though the only absolutely certain fact is that he did not live to the end of World War II. The Soviets recalled him to Russia and he obeyed, despite the judicial murder of many of his colleagues among communist spies. Several stories about his death have come down in history, with none fully corroborated by documentation. One version asserts that Deutsch parachuted into Third Reich territory, fell into SS hands, and suffered execution by firing squad as the spy he undoubtedly was. This narrative put the scene of his demise in Austria.

According to a second story, Deutsch requested enlistment in the Red Army to fight the Germans directly, but Moscow had other uses for his talents. In 1942, the NKVD sent him on board the SS *Donbass* on a journey to New York, ordering him to repeat his successful recruitment efforts in the United States. However, on November 7th, 1942, the Kriegsmarine destroyer Z-27 under Karl Ernst Smidt intercepted the SS Donbass in the Barents Sea and attacked the tanker vigorously. Though the Soviet crew fired their small deck guns and machine guns defiantly, the powerful German vessel – armed almost like a light cruiser – launched three torpedoes which blasted the Donbass in half. Deutsch sustained mortal injuries during the attack, though he managed to help several men escape the sinking vessel before dying of his wounds. Z-27 rescued the 15 survivors from the water, though 33 others died in the attack.

While Z-27 did indeed since the SS *Donbass* precisely as described, there is no separate corroboration of Deutsch's presence on the ship. He is not mentioned on the commemorative plaque of those who lost their lives during the sinking. It remains possible that like other Soviet spies who returned at the time, Deutsch spent his last hours screaming in an NKVD torture cell before being marched out and shot, and that his friends – including Philby – later concocted comforting tales of a more heroic death.

Perhaps not surprisingly, the spies themselves found the Soviets difficult masters. While they supplied huge quantities of accurate information, the Soviets remained highly suspicious of this wealth of intelligence and acted on less than they might for several years. Two reasons motivated this suspicion. First, the Soviets held MI6 in much higher esteem than it in fact deserved, holding it to be an impenetrable fortress run with the precision of an elite military unit. The idea that the formidable British Empire admitted men and women into its intelligence service on the basis of family and university attendance, with practically no background checks, seemed absurd to the fatally paranoid NKVD. The nature of English society utterly escaped the minds of Stalin's henchmen.

Second, the fact that Philby's spying indicated the Soviet Union held very low priority among English spying targets deeply affronted the Soviets. They imagined this to be the British giving false information to the Cambridge Five, concealing a massive spying effort. The mighty Soviet intelligence apparatus fell victim to its own amateurish vanity. In time, however, this attitude reversed itself and the Soviets recognized the value of Philby's intelligence – once he had betrayed hundreds of anticommunists in Europe to their deaths.

The Cambridge spy ring started passing along intelligence to the Soviets through the new handlers sent after the purge, each focusing on their own department. Kim Philby had already cheerfully and promptly spied on his father, his friends, and his wife at the behest of the Soviets, and now moved on to grander targets.

While he assisted MI6 with efforts to disrupt Nazi Germany's Abwehr intelligence efforts in Spain and Portugal, he also carried out several tasks for his Soviet masters. His office building stood next to Central Registry of the SIS Archives. The Registry represented an almost incredible gathering of top-secret material, since it contained a complete library of every British agent and spy in the world, complete with all available data on them, ranging from their names and code-names to descriptions of their personality and background.

Penetrating this archive could, without exaggeration, enable a spy to betray any British agent alive to a foreign power. The Soviets ordered Philby to do precisely that as proof of his loyalty. Philby found the task of gaining free access to this storehouse of information that held the fates and lives of thousands of people quite easy, even though he ought never to have been permitted access without proper authorization from on high. As Philby described with more than a hint of sarcasm: "Bill Woodfield, who was in charge of [the Central Registry], had become quite a friend of mine. I have been told that magenta is the only colour that the rainbow lacks. If so, Bill's face would be out of place in the rainbow. He had a liking for pink gins, which I shared, and prudish appreciation of dirty stories. We used to foregather often to discuss office politics [...] This friendly connection paid off, and I was usually in a position to get files rather more quickly and easily than many of my colleagues." (Philby, 2003, 60-61).

Philby tested the strength of his alcohol-soaked "friendship" by first requesting the source-books for agents in Spain and Portugal. This would give him plausible deniability if challenged, since his official tasks currently focused on fighting the Abwehr in precisely those nations. Woodfield handed the books over promptly and without question. Accordingly, Philby asked for those listing all agents in the Soviet Union, and the purple-faced Woodfield again obliged despite the fact that Philby had no remote reason for needing access to the information.

Philby cracked open the source-books and discovered that the English had no spies in the Soviet Union, only a tiny handful of Polish informers not dignified with agent status. He reported this to the Soviets, sending them into a fury and causing them to suspect Philby had double-crossed them.

However, Philby in fact told the truth. The British had neglected to install spies in the USSR just as the Germans – with no intention or desire to conquer or even fight against England or its Empire – did not place a single spy in Britain prior to the outbreak of war. Philby had no qualms about betraying his own countrymen to possible capture, torture, and death, but truly lacked anyone to betray.

The other members of the cell had their own contributions to offer. Though often overlooked in accounts of the Cambridge Five as a relatively unimportant member, John Cairncross provided the Soviet Union with some of its most valuable intelligence during the war. Working among the British code-breakers at Bletchley Park, Cairncross provided his handler, Boris Krotenschield or "Krechin," with decrypted messages and information the British did not pass on to the Soviets.

The English withheld this information because they feared that German moles in the NKVD would reveal the code-breaking program and cause the Nazis to change their codes, with disastrous consequences for Allied wartime intelligence. This information had a crucial effect on the massive tank battle at the Kursk Salient. Cairncross obtained and passed on "technical data about the new German Tiger tank. [...] Its principal feature was the thickness of its armor, which could not be pierced by our shells. The Germans were convinced at the time that Russian cannons would be powerless to halt this new tank. Thanks to the documents obtained by Cairncross, we were able to analyze the thickness of the armor and assess the quality of the steel – and then to manufacture armor-piercing shells capable of knocking out the Tiger." (Modin, 1994, 113).

Furthermore, Cairncross gave the Soviets reams of data on Luftwaffe airbases near the Kursk Salient. This enabled the Red Army Air Force to strike the Germans repeatedly before the offensive, claiming the destruction of 500 Luftwaffe aircraft on the ground. While probably exaggerated (as the kill claims of every nation's air forces tend to be), the damage wreaked on German air assets contributed materially to the failure of the Germans to pincer the Kursk Salient and destroy the vast numbers of Soviet troops inside. Air support for "Operation Citadel" still existed following the Soviet raids, but did not have the overwhelming punch it could have mustered just a few weeks prior. The Soviets awarded Cairncross the Order of the Red Banner for this espionage coup. The NKVD sent the physical medal to London, where Krechin presented it to his agent. Cairncross handled the medal reverently, before Krechin packed it up and sent it on to Moscow again lest it be discovered and give away Cairncross' Soviet connection.

Cairncross and Donald Maclean also provided the KGB with information on the Manhattan Project. While they lacked access to the critical scientific data, they passed on all American and British secret communications about the progress of the atom bomb's development throughout the entire research period. Maclean received an assignment to the Combined Policy Committee, and "a top-secret mission to coordinate the American Manhattan Project to develop the atomic bomb with the British Tube Alloys project. [...] It is no overstatement to say that the KGB was able to follow the political evolution of the Western atomic program from its genesis right through to the first test detonation near Alamogordo, New Mexico." (Modin, 1994, 118). While this data might seem of lesser importance, it in fact provided the Soviets with confirmation of an atom bomb's feasibility and allowed them to accelerate the timetable of finding scientists they could subvert to obtain the scientific secrets for themselves. Without the efforts of the Cambridge Five, the nuclear weapons deployed at Hiroshima and Nagasaki might well have come as a total surprise to the USSR, and their own nuclear program might consequently have been delayed by several more years.

A constant ferment of espionage activity occurred in Istanbul, Turkey, the colorful and utterly corrupt capital of a neutral power located at the juncture between the Soviet Union, the Third Reich's Balkan territories, and the British Empire's holdings in the Middle East and

Mediterranean regions. It provided a point of contact where agents and defectors could most easily move in and out of the various "empires," while provocateurs and diplomats could attempt to bring Turkey into the war on side or another. MI6 sent Philby's friend Nicolas Elliot, along with his female secretary Elizabeth Holberton, to Turkey by way of Palestine. On the way, a passionate romance blossomed between the cheerful, resourceful Elliot and the charming, clever Holberton. They soon formed an inseparable couple and would be married in Istanbul by no less than the Apostolic Delegate to Turkey, Angelo Giuseppe Roncalli, the future Pope John XXIII.

Pope John XXIII

All of the major powers maintained a large intelligence staff in Istanbul, a swarming anthill of agents of many nationalities and allegiances, or none at all. An even larger contingent of minor hangers-on made the city their home, including both Turks and men and women from most of the nations of Europe as well as further abroad. These bit players in the perilous game of international espionage sought to enrich themselves however they could, wheedling or stealing secrets from one set of agents to sell to another. Bribery flourished and obscure people sometimes made astounding intelligence coups.

Istanbul had the heady feeling of a spy thriller, with dangerous or studious agents rubbing shoulders amid a sea of cheap or glitzy hotels, casinos, bars, bordellos, and diplomatic villas. The city housed Abwehr men from Nazi Germany, NKVD agents, Britishers from MI6, Italian spies, and agents of Imperial Japan, each with their staffs of helpers, guards, clerks, and other personnel.

Despite the deadly earnest of the spying and their intense efforts to defeat or outwit one another, the agents maintained a surprising friendly attitude towards their enemies – though laced with the underlying aggression of competing sportsmen. The Third Reich's ambassador Franz von Papen attended Elliott and Holberton's wedding with several of his officers in tow. On the other hand, matters could also turn lethal. The Germans blew up a British agent with a suitcase bomb shortly before Elliott's arrival; the NKVD sent a suitcase bomb to von Papen via a Macedonian student, who tarried too long on his journey – the bomb exploded just as he entered the restaurant where von Papen was dining, blowing the student to pieces but only slightly wounding the German; and one of Elliott's Turkish informants gave him a third such device that Colonel Tateishi, the leader of the Japanese agents, had provided to him in order to blow up a train, but which the Turk sold at an immense profit to Elliott instead, and the Englishman then disposed of before it could explode.

Istanbul in 1943 yielded an intelligence coup which allowed Philby to return to the good graces of his suspicious Soviet masters. A new Abwehr agent, Erich Vermehren, arrived in the Turkish city, while his wife Elisabeth remained behind in Germany as a quasi-hostage against his good behavior. Nevertheless, Vermehren intended to defect if he could figure out a way to bring his wife with him. A pious Catholic, Vermehren objected to both Hitler and the Soviets, and wanted to put the British in touch with the Catholic resistance who opposed both the Nazis and the communists.

Vermehren met with Elliott on December 23rd, 1943, immediately feeling reassured by the Britisher's presence. The Elliotts, husband and wife, served the nervous German defector dinner, after which Elliott masterfully assured Vermehren that he would perform a great service against the Nazis, while telling him he could no longer change his mind without being killed by the Gestapo. Caught between hope and fear, Vermehren agreed to give the British all the information he could about the secret Catholic networks.

Elisabeth Vermehren managed to fly to Istanbul thanks to the good offices of a friend in the Nazi hierarchy. Since her presence in a foreign city with her husband represented an illegal act under Abwehr rules, Elliott needed to act quickly. The British staged an "abduction" in which disguised men very publicly seized the Vermehrens and dragged them into an unmarked car. The English took the couple to the Turkish shore under cover of darkness and sent them to Cairo by a fast motor launch. From there, they boarded a ship to England. Two more German Abwehr agents defected within days.

Once ensconced safely in England, the Vermehrens underwent extensive debriefing by Elliot and Philby, describing the network of anti-Nazi and anti-communist German Catholics in great detail. Though both husband and wife subjected the two agents to lengthy religious lectures which secretly drove both men mad with impatience, they nevertheless provided their British hosts with a wealth of invaluable information. Erich Vermehren, with Teutonic thoroughness, gave the two young Englishmen a long list of activists he had prepared, containing not only hundreds of names but also the full addresses and occupations of these men and women.

Delighted at this prize, Philby forwarded the information to the NKVD. This gave the communists a complete list of the anti-communists in Germany. As the Red Army surged into German territory at the end of the war, NKVD troops and agents accompanying them carried Vermehren's list among the documents listing Germans meant for elimination. Using this resource, they ferreted out every last individual on the roster who happened to be in the area occupied by Soviet troops.

British attempts to contact them postwar proved fruitless because the Soviet secret police and intelligence forces had done their work with merciless thoroughness, locating and shooting hundreds of anti-communist Germans and thousands of their family members to be certain of eliminating a possible obstacle to their rule.

As victory over the Third Reich became ever more certain in late 1944 and early 1945, the focus of the Cambridge Five's operations shifted in that field, too. They continued to pass on decrypted German military communications from Bletchley Park, but communications between Churchill and Roosevelt, and, later, Churchill and Truman began taking center stage as the Western Allies and Soviet Union commenced serious negotiations regarding the postwar order in Europe and the world.

The information provided by the various members of the Five enabled Stalin and Molotov to piece together much of the thought process, concerns, and potential weak points in their dealings with the Soviet strongman before they ever came to the negotiating table. This allowed Stalin and his close advisers to determine that Truman did not share Churchill's qualms about the fate of Poland, as just a single example.

Donald Maclean, while simultaneously providing as much data as he could about the atom bomb from his posting in Washington DC, also managed to procure copies of almost all the secret telegrams passing back and forth between the heads of state of the USA and UK. Maclean's wife and son stayed in New York City, which gave him a pretext to travel there frequently – actually to meet with his NKVD handlers, who then relayed all his purloined information to Moscow.

The Cold War

Immediately after the close of World War II, the Istanbul spy scene very nearly led to the unmasking of the Cambridge Five – an exposure which might have well have resulted in their hanging for treason. Only Kim Philby's personal intervention, which led directly to the kidnapping, torture and execution of a Soviet defector and his wife by the NKVD, spared the five men from disgrace and the hangman's noose.

A piece of careful maneuvering by Philby paid off handsomely in this instance. Rather cheekily, Philby approached the head of MI6, the tough, driven, and stereotypically British Sir Stewart Menzies and proposed that the agency should form a new anti-Soviet section, Section IX. Menzies heartily agreed, immediately ordering the organization of an anti-communist branch of MI6 and choosing Felix Cowgill as the prime candidate for its new chief.

This appointment represented a setback for Philby, who clearly urged the creation of an anti-communist office so that, as its first advocate, he would receive leadership of it. This would put the branch specifically charged with ferreting out traitors like himself in the hands of a traitor, ensuring that Section IX would be a complete failure at its task. However, Menzies, naturally unaware of the plot, almost wrecked Philby's plan by intending to place a different individual at the section's head.

Resourceful and undaunted – and no doubt motivated by a desperate urge to survive – Philby set about fatally undermining Cowgill's candidature. He did this by seeking out Cowgill's numerous enemies (due to his abrasive personality rather than professional failings) and prompting them to work together against Cowgill. He managed to enlist Valentine Vivian, liaison with MI5 and head of the SIS, in the anti-Cowgill posse. Philby also stirred up MI5 against Cowgill: "Apart from Dick White, who was still personally affable, the rest of the personnel of MI5 knew Cowgill only as an antagonist in inter-office strife. Even White described him, kindly, as 'an awkward bugger.'" (Philby, 2003, 98).

Philby continued prodding and backbiting, stirring up as many old adversaries of Cowgill as he could find. He worked with the indefatigable energy of a man who knows that dangling from a gallows may well be the price of failure. Finally, the breakthrough came when Vivian decided to write to Menzies directly: "The ordeal virtually ended one day when Vivian summoned me, and asked me to read a minute he had written to the Chief. It was of inordinate length and laced with quotations from *Hamlet*. It traced the sorry story of Cowgill's quarrels, and argued that a radical change must be made before the transition to peacetime conditions. My name was put forward as a successor to Currie. Cowgill's candidature for the appointment was specifically excluded. My own suitability for the post was explained in flattering detail." (Philby, 2003, 98).

Menzies heeded the note from Vivian and replaced Cowgill with Philby as the incoming head of the new department. Rather than dispute the choice or seek a different post in MI6, Cowgill flew into a rage and resigned from the service, clearing away one of the men with the best chance of detecting the Cambridge Five.

In September 1945, Philby's maneuvering paid off with his first miraculous survival. Konstantin Volkov, a Soviet consular official in Istanbul, decided to defect to the West, laying his plans very carefully before making his move. He compiled a list of 250 Soviet agents in Britain, including all of the Cambridge Five and their handlers, and 314 Soviet spies in Turkey. He also obtained copies of a large number of documents sent to Moscow by infiltrators in British intelligence – no doubt including many directly traceable to the Cambridge Five – and placed these in a suitcase in a vacant Moscow apartment.

Volkov and his wife Zoya then visited the British vice-consul in Istanbul, Hamilton Page, recently wounded by that favorite tool of agents operating in Turkey, a suitcase bomb. With Zoya in a state of terror over what would befall them should the NKVD discover their visit, and Volkov almost equally agitated, the Russian demanded 50,000 pounds in exchange for the information he would provide, which he would hand over only when safely on English territory.

He said that he knew the names of multiple English traitors operating inside MI6 and other intelligence agencies for the benefit of the Soviets, and even referred to one who, with the clarity of hindsight, could only have been Kim Philby himself directing Section IX, the anti-Soviet branch of MI6: "I know, for instance, that one of these agents is fulfilling the functions of head of a section of the British counter-espionage service in London."

With almost nightmarish ill fortune from Volkov's perspective, this explosive and invaluable intelligence coup revolted the British ambassador, Sir Maurice Peterson. Recoiling in Victorian disgust at the notion of spying, he forwarded the information to precisely the worst place to send it – MI6.

Sir Stewart Menzies received the report of Volkov's planned defection and the vital information it would provide. Delighted at this potential coup, he passed it on to the bright young head of the counter-Soviet Section IX, the impeccably credentialed Kim Philby. Philby recounted his shock at the material delivered to his office: "Two Soviet agents in the Foreign Office, one head of a counter-espionage organization in London! I stared at the papers rather longer than necessary to compose my thoughts. I rejected the idea of suggesting caution […] It would be useless in the short run, and might possibly compromise me at a later date. The only course was to put a bold face on it." (Philby, 2003, 119).

Philby went to Menzies and suggested that a matter so crucial could only be handled by him personally, and that Menzies should send him to Istanbul. The head of MI6 agreed, and a series of flights (avoiding Axis airspace) brought Philby to Turkey. At the same time, MI6 detected a massive increase in Soviet encoded radio traffic between London and Moscow, followed within an hour by a huge spike in radio traffic between Moscow and Istanbul. Astoundingly, Menzies failed to connect the arrival of Volkov's explosive material with this highly unusual increase in signals.

When Philby arrived on September 26th, he immediately spoke to Hamilton Page about contacting Volkov, pretending great eagerness to meet the defector and remove him to safety. Page, also ready to begin – and in fact, marveling inwardly at Philby's incompetence at not arriving sooner, according to his later statements – picked up the telephone and called the Soviet consulate. At this point, matters took an eerie and sinister turn, according to Guy Liddell, another British intelligence officer on the scene: "The telephone was answered by the Soviet Consul General on the first occasion and on the second by a man speaking English claiming to be Wolkoff [ie Volkov] but [who] clearly was not. Finally contact was made with the Russian telephone operator." (Andrew, 2009, 345).

Page listened in bewilderment to the voice of the young woman on the other end of the telephone who, in heavily accented English, told him that Volkov was "out." She then hung up the telephone. The Englishman, undeterred, called once again. The same young woman answered and this time told him "Volkov is in Moscow" – the actual truth in this case. Totally baffled, Page drove to the Soviet consulate. Though the Soviets allowed him to enter the outer offices, every individual he spoke to now assured him that nobody named Volkov ever been in Istanbul, that Konstantin Volkov did not work for the consulate, and that none of them had even heard of a man named Volkov.

In fact, by the time Page walked into the consulate, the Volkovs were probably already dead. Several days earlier, tipped off by Philby's communications, NKVD agents seized the couple, drugged them, wrapped them in bandages like mummies, and strapped them onto stretchers. Thus immobilized, the pair found themselves carried past lackadaisical Turkish airport inspectors as injured Russians in need of urgent medical care in the Motherland and flown out of Turkey. However, upon their arrival, the NKVD took them to the Lubyanka cellars rather than a hospital. There, Volkov and his wife underwent "brutal" torture to learn what they had divulged. Volkov confessed every detail of his planned defection.

Once satisfied they had learned everything, the NKVD shot the pair and cremated their bodies. However, their vengeance did not stop with the deaths of Volkov and his wife. The NKVD destroyed the official files about them, or at least hid them so thoroughly in secret archives that no researchers in post-Soviet Russia have located them to date. All photographs of the couple similarly underwent destruction, obliterating their visual memory as much as the USSR's considerable power allowed. Finally, the NKVD arrested and secretly executed all of their relatives, eradicating their families from the Earth.

Philby, later gloating in his memoirs that he had disposed of Volkov, whom he termed a "nasty piece of work," wired Menzies that Volkov had inexplicably disappeared. He advanced the theory that Volkov had betrayed himself while drunk. Emulating his fictional scenario, Philby stopped in Rome for a massive, three-day alcoholic binge with his friend, the American agent James Jesus Angleton. He then returned to England with his reputation surprisingly intact and Menzies' trust in him unshaken.

The Cambridge Five had survived their first major crisis. However, from that moment on until his own defection to the USSR, Philby lived in a state of constant fear, knowing that not only could another defector bring equally ruinous information at any time, but that an alert British intelligence officer looking over the records could easily spot how the chain of events surrounding Volkov's disappearance pointed squarely at Philby's guilt as an agent of the Soviets.

Philby's post at the head of Section IX now made him the most important of the Cambridge Five and their de facto leader. As the man directly responsible for clandestine operations against the Soviets, ranging from managing networks of spies in the Soviet Union to handling the training and deployment of small bands of anti-communist patriots from the Soviet-occupied countries of the Balkans and Eastern Europe in the hopes of launching independence movements in those nations.

The Soviets knew of every British plan and action, along with the identity and location of every one of the agents recruited by the English, thanks to Kim Philby. However, in order to avoid unmasking their highly placed mole, they did not act directly to crush the MI6 intelligence network in Russia. The Soviets left some of the agents free, feeding them disinformation or ensuring that they never acquired really sensitive data. Others they turned, using them as double agents through whom they fed real but essentially useless information, again to avoid compromising Philby.

Valentine Vivian received another glaring clue that Philby might be a Soviet agent at this time, but again ignored it with characteristic obtuseness. Philby, separated from Litzi since 1936, now requested Vivian's permission to track down his former wife and divorce her so that he could marry Aileen Furse, the secretly mentally disordered woman who captivated him mid-war, concealing her tendencies towards self-harm and pyromania. In doing so, he admitted Litzi's status as a Viennese communist activist, since she now lived in East Germany and he would need to travel there to secure a divorce.

Vivian had the background of Litzi checked and MI6 confirmed her as a Comintern agent and Soviet spy. Nevertheless, he cheerfully granted Philby's request. Philby and Litzi (now living with another man in any case) officially divorced and Philby married Aileen. The fact that the head of the anti-Soviet Section IX had been married for decades to a confirmed communist fanatic and Soviet secret agent seemingly failed to perturb Vivian in the slightest.

In 1946, Philby also received two medals, one openly, the other in secret. The English awarded him the Order of the British Empire for his wartime intelligence serve, while, unannounced, the Soviets gave him the Order of the Red Banner for his intelligence work against the British as well as the Germans.

Nicolas Elliott, Philby's friend and firm anti-communist, now headed British intelligence operations in Switzerland, and Philby made a point of visiting him whenever he traveled to the continent. While he undoubtedly enjoyed Elliott's cheerful, joking company, this also enabled him to keep an eye on this dangerously intelligent agent working against Philby's Soviet masters with genuine dedication and patriotism.

Philby, carrying out his double role, also visited the American agent and strange eccentric James Angleton in Rome. Angleton, another dedicated anticommunist, represented another adversary Philby needed to keep a close eye on. The American actually proved successful at building several important intelligence networks, but also hired a series of untrustworthy characters, damaging both the value of his information and his career. One such, who eventually forged a huge volume of fake "secret Vatican communications to cheat Angleton the US government out of considerable money for his services, was "Virgilio Scattolini, a corpulent Italian journalist who wrote bestselling, semi-pornographic novels, including one entitled, rather unenticingly, *Amazons in the Bidet."* (MacIntyre, 2015, 110).

Angleton fully trusted Philby, ill-advisedly telling him that he had successfully bugged the offices of Italian Communist Party chief Palmiro Togliatti. Togliatti in fact worked for the Soviets, and Philby's latest handler, Boris Krötenschield, duly apprised the KGB of the bugging. Angleton therefore never learned anything of much use from his surveillance devices thanks to his confiding in Philby.

Several of the Cambridge Five now left the intelligence service for peacetime occupations, though in some cases this enabled them to provide ongoing secret information. The flamboyant Guy Burgess became the secretary of Hector MacNeil, an important Minister of State in Clement Attlee's postwar Foreign Office. This allowed him to copy huge amounts of correspondence, giving the KGB (now the agency responsible for handling foreign espionage) reams of communications between the British and American governments as well as other powers.

While these agents continued their work, the KGB struggled with a problem of their own – the inability to keep large numbers of operatives in the field to handle the spies in the West. Peacetime greatly increased the risk of defection among KGB operatives confronted by the material temptations of the western republics. Simultaneously, the few highly loyal, patriotic agents sent abroad longed continually to return to Russia, and found themselves under immense workload due to being understaffed. The KGB withdrew these operatives once it appeared the strain might overwhelm them, but then judged it best to keep them in Russia rather than send them to foreign parts again.

Though little remembered today, determined resistance movements continued to fight the Soviet occupiers in most of the Eastern Bloc countries in the years immediately following World

War II. The insurgency in Ukraine, led by Ukrainian SS troops led by the Germans, proved a particular thorn in the USSR's side, with the last holdouts not quashed until 1950 and thousands killed in total on both sides.

Resistance movements also continued for several years in the Baltic states, ethnically and nationally distinct and most with a strong sense of national tradition and pride. Though much smaller than the Ukrainian conflict, these struggles still claimed hundreds of lives. Intelligence provided by Philby proved central to Soviet strategy in the struggle against these partisan bands, as the KGB operative Yuri Modin described: "The British had a penchant for parachuting agents into the Baltic countries, where there was already a strong, well-organized resistance. Philby gave us details of every operation in Lithuania and Estonia; they usually involved arms deliveries or the infiltration of combatants or messengers via Sweden or the Baltic. We knew who was coming, and when, and we neutralized these spies and saboteurs; most were arrested and imprisoned." (Modin, 1994, 127).

Yugoslavia's evasion of inclusion in the Soviet empire under the wily Marshal Tito provided hope that other Balkan countries might detach from the USSR if correctly "primed." The British concentrated their efforts heavily on Albania, where a ruthless communist dictatorship combined with a fiery, independent people seemed to offer the highest chances of starting a popular revolt. MI6 set their sights a similar program in Georgia also.

Accordingly, in 1947 they moved their "best man" – Kim Philby – and his family close to the scene of the action, installing him in considerable style in Turkey at Beylerbeyi. A group of five intelligence officers accompanied him to form his core staff, and he also inherited the local intelligence assets built up during World War II by Nicolas Elliott and other MI6 men operating in and around Istanbul.

Philby would use Guy Burgess, still in England, to send his reports on to Moscow. This avoided the risks inherent in contacting a Soviet operative directly in Turkey, a land swarming with spies and informers.

1947 also witnessed the founding of the CIA (Central Intelligence Agency), to replace the wartime OSS. The CIA and MI6 set about training the large number of Albanian and Georgian anti-communist exiles then in western cities as guerrilla fighters, ready to stir up popular resistance movements in their home countries.

Soon, the British judged themselves ready to insert the first two Georgian counter-revolutionaries across the Turkish border. A pair of enthusiastic, brave, and naive young men, one of them identified only as Rukhadzhe, the other anonymous to history, arrived in Turkey and traveled to the eastern border in Philby's company.

Philby had already given exact details of the plan, Operation Climber, to the Soviets. He therefore took his charges to a distant spot on the border where the KGB had prearranged a "welcoming committee" for the hapless Georgians. Philby, on stage for his agents, gave the two men radios, bags of gold coins, and firearms before they slipped away into the darkness. Almost immediately, the waiting Soviet agents opened fire on the pair, killing the anonymous Georgian instantly. The British glimpsed Rukhadzhe trying to escape from his KGB pursuers, but they soon captured him. His captors took him to the nearest town, tortured him to discover what he knew, then shot him.

Philby had arranged this catastrophic failure in the hope that MI6 would entirely abandon the idea of sending provocateurs into Soviet territory. In this, it ultimately failed. However, it did delay the next attempts for some time as the British and Americans sought to prepare their next nationalist partisans more carefully. The success of the Soviets in fomenting communist revolution in Greece (eventually quashed) provided a strong catalyst for a retaliatory measure, as the minutes of the Russia Committee meeting from November 25th, 1948 reveal "offensive operations might be best started in a small area […] Would it not be possible to start a civil war behind the Iron Curtain and, by careful assistance, produce a state of affairs in Albania similar to the state of affairs that the Russians had produced in Greece? […] our aim should certainly be to liberate the countries within the Soviet orbit short of war." (Hamrick, 2004, 194-195).

In the meantime, Philby, suffering from increasing marital difficulties but still buoyant as ever, found himself posted to Washington DC in the United States by MI6. Here he renewed his close acquaintance with his old friend James Jesus Angleton, now busy in the thick of the counter-communist covert operations. The two went drinking frequently, and Angleton shared practically all his knowledge of the situation with drunken candor, finding a seemingly sympathetic listener in the charming Philby.

Philby also hosted many parties during which he and Aileen plied their FBI and CIA agent guests with immense quantities of alcohol. This also naturally loosened tongues, as did Philby's confiding manner combined with his unfailing humor and wit. While the Britisher produced first-class information for his Soviet masters, it received third-class treatment at best. Soviet arrangements to transmit this trove of data remained very poor, with the intelligence sent by mail through Valeriy Makayev, a KGB agent in New York City who spent more time pursuing sexual adventures with ballerinas than doing the work that Moscow paid him for.

Some historical doubt remains how useful Philby's intelligence proved to the Soviets, sent via mail rather than telegraph or radio and therefore extremely slow. Nevertheless, the fact remains that Angleton told Philby about practically every operation in Lithuania, Estonia, Ukraine, Albania, and Georgia during the late 1940s, and that every one of these attempted insertions of nationalists and freedom fighters ended with the brave but luckless men either killed immediately in a firefight, or captured, tortured until they broke, given a show trial at which they apologized profusely for propaganda purposes, and then vanished into the prisons and gulags of the USSR.

Beyond betraying every detail of all the counter-Soviet operations in the USSR's conquered countries, Philby used his trained and acute mind to memorize entire documents relating to all SIS and CIA plans for espionage and counter-espionage if a war began with the Soviet Union. All of the careful pre-planning by both agencies soon found its way to the KGB in Moscow.

Had the Cold War gone hot in the late 1940s, the Soviets would have enjoyed the same absolute intelligence advantage over the westerners as the Western Allies had over the Third Reich when they decrypted Germany's Enigma codes, with likely devastating results for Britain and America. A CIA officer, Miles Copeland, later summed up the situation effectively: "What it comes to, is that when you look at that whole period from 1944 to 1951 – leaving out anything [Philby] picked up at other times – the entire Western intelligence effort, which was pretty big, was what you might call minus advantage. We'd have been better off doing nothing (Holzman, 2008, 125).

Just as the Albanians had been "set up" by the Soviets to betray themselves to capture, torture, and death, so Philby's spying transformed all the effort made by the CIA and SIS to prepare for World War III into a death trap. The leader of the Cambridge Five had served his masters well. Had war erupted at that time, all the ingenuity and forethought of the western intelligence services would have been turned abruptly against them and become a possibly fatal detriment to their own nations.

At around this time, Guy Burgess joined Philby in Washington DC. Philby put his friend and fellow spy up at his house, causing Aileen – who had shaken off her mental peculiarities for a time in the new and exciting venue – to fall into a fresh decline.

Burgess proved even more obnoxious and dissolute than previously, racking up speeding tickets – and insulting the officers who pulled him over for speeding in the most colorfully obscene manner he could – drinking to excess, boasting of his homosexual exploits, and amusing himself by insulting Philby's American guests so grossly that one of them, William Harvey, punched the Burgess in the face, which the alcoholic spy found even more hilarious.

The Cambridge Five Unmasked

At this moment, on January 19th, 1951, with Philby's clandestine star in the ascendant and his greatest intelligence triumphs coming thick and fast, the end of the Cambridge Five drew closer with remarkable speed. Even as Bill Harvey punched Burgess at Philby's January's "party from hell" for drawing an obscene caricature of his wife with her vagina exposed, men in the SIS and CIA had begun to close the net, thanks to an intelligence coup known as the Venona decrypts.

Starting in 1943, British and American intelligence intercepted thousands of thousands of encoded NKVD, GRU, and KGB messages as part of the "Venona Project." The Soviets used a one-time pad encryption method which would have been unbreakable without human error. However, the office printing the pads created 35,000 duplicates during World War II, leading to repeated use of some pads and the possibility of cracking the code using this error as a starting point.

A young American man with a genius for cryptography, Meredith Knox Gardner, received the task of leading the code-breakers working on the Soviet intercepts. A cousin of the political commentator Patrick Buchanan, Gardner worked diligently for decades at the grueling task of translating parts of the Venona intercepts vulnerable to decryption.

In late 1950 and early 1951, Gardner's efforts began to pay juicy dividends. The very day following Philby's "party from hell," January 20th, 1951, the US government indicted Alger Hiss for perjury, based on secret Venona decrypts. On January 23rd, Klaus Fuchs admitted to providing nuclear secrets to the Soviet Union. Philby knew of the Venona decrypts – indeed, he pretended friendship with Meredith Gardner and watched him at work frequently – and these developments put him on high alert.

He had reason for alarm. The decrypts had already revealed that an agent code-named Homer (actually Donald Maclean) sent many secret communications about the atom bomb to the Soviets during the Manhattan Project. Shortly after Fuchs' fall, Gardner decrypted a fateful June 1944 Soviet message. This message stated that "Homer's" pregnant wife lived in New York City with her mother.

Like hounds on the scent, MI5's best minds threw themselves on this clue and reviewed the backgrounds of all potential spies with access to the Manhattan Project communications. Almost at once, they discovered that in 1944 Donald Maclean's Melinda Marling lived in New York City with her mother, and was pregnant at the time. Maclean had already been under surveillance for some time as one of nine possible moles in British intelligence. Now MI5 closed in on their man.

Philby racked his brains on how to warn Maclean without revealing his own Soviet allegiance. Two circumstances favored him. MI5, appalled at the magnitude of Gardner's discovery, hesitated for a remarkable five weeks before taking action against Maclean, hoping to acquire more proof of his treason. And Guy Burgess' absurd antics finally caused enough embarrassment for his recall to London.

Philby made Burgess his messenger to Maclean, warning him to flee. Burgess would visit Maclean at his office on arrival, a natural thing for men working for the same department to do, and give him a piece of paper instructing him to defect to the USSR.

Burgess duly traveled to England, where he informed Yuri Modin of the whole situation, in a state approaching chattering panic. Modin contacted KGB headquarters and secured rapid consent for the defection of Maclean before the British arrested him. Melinda Maclean, who had known since before her marriage to him that Donald Maclean worked as a spy for the Soviets, urged her husband to escape while he still could.

Getting Maclean out of the country proved easier than might be imagined. In almost absurdly stereotypical fashion, the men and women of MI5 now following Maclean everywhere watched him like a hawk – but only during regular office hours on weekdays. At the end of the workday, MI5's agents simply went home, leaving Maclean unobserved throughout the night until they returned to work the following morning. Similarly, surveillance of the suspect ended on Friday evening and did not resume until Monday morning the following week!

As it happened, MI5 issued an interrogation warrant for Maclean on Friday, May 25th, 1951. Due to their obsession with a civilized work week, however, the agents postponed detaining Maclean until Monday, May 28th. Modin decided on May 25th to smuggle Maclean out of the country.

Briefly puzzled at how to accomplish this on short notice, Modin learned from Anthony Blunt about British weekend cruise ships that sojourned along the French coast: "These vessels left England on Friday evenings, put in at two or three Continental ports over the weekend, and returned […] Monday morning. […] immigration controls on these excursions were practically nonexistent. I was astonished by this, but Blunt explained that such cruises were particularly favored by businessmen and senior civil servants, people who might want to spend a few days in isolation with a secretary or a mistress. For this reason, the immigration services showed unique restraint." (Modin, 1994, 205).

However, the KGB made a fatal blunder with their plans. Rather than sending one of several available Russian operatives with Maclean to aid him in slipping through Europe, the Russians ordered Modin to send Burgess with Maclean to the USSR. Philby had extracted a promise from Burgess to avoid defecting, knowing that Burgess' flight to the Soviet Union would point major suspicion back at him.

Modin revealed that Burgess would accompany Maclean, and Burgess objected feebly. However, he soon agreed, convincing himself that the Soviets would allow him to return and stay in England, thus keeping his cover and that of Philby intact.

Burgess and Maclean boarded the *Falaise* in haste a few minutes before midnight on May 25th. Once they landed in France, a few short train trips took them to Switzerland, where they acquired fake passports at the Soviet embassy. These allowed them to fly first to Sweden, then on to Soviet territory in Czechoslovakia, landing in Prague before the British even realized their absence.

On Monday, May 18th, MI5 searched in vain for Maclean. Their search, however, revealed Burgess' car abandoned at a wharf in Southampton used by cruise ships. This news caused a shockwave through both the British and American intelligence establishments. William Harvey, still seething over Burgess' insults to his wife at Philby's dinner party, pounced on the opportunity to torpedo Philby, whom he suspected in any case. He sent a message that "traced Philby's recent career and contacts, and asserted that Philby had to be a Soviet agent... Smith immediately shipped off the damning Philby material to 'C,' Stewart Menzies, in London, accompanied by a typically uncluttered cover letter: 'Fire Philby or we break off the intelligence relationship.'" (Holzman, 2008, 124).

Philby reacted to the situation by immediately burying his Soviet-made and supplied camera deep in the woods. He then remained at his post to brazen out the inevitable inquiry. He obeyed the summons to return to London for questioning in early June 1951, never to return to the United States.

On June 12th, Philby reported to MI5 and spent several hours talking with Richard White, who conducted a very friendly and proper but thorough interrogation of the Soviet spy. At the same time, the leadership of MI6 closed ranks to support Philby against MI5's suspicions and the open accusations issuing from the CIA in the wake of Harvey's report. Elliott, returning from Switzerland, defended his friend and colleague fiercely.

Nevertheless, Richard White conducted a second interview with Philby, during which he grew convinced that Philby had a high probability of spying for the Soviets. Armed with more information now, White brought up Philby's Comintern agent wife, his early association with communists, and the nearly incredible string of failures in attempts to smuggle patriotic resistance fighters into Eastern Europe and the Balkans. Philby offered an extravagant string of excuses which only deepened White's suspicions.

Though still considered legally innocent, Philby obviously could not remain at MI6 during the investigation of his possible treason. He accordingly moved to a small country house with his family, where MI5 agents and police kept a continuous watch on his movements. This time, there would be no cessation of surveillance after normal working hours and on the weekend.

Philby, guessing correctly that MI5 had wired the house thoroughly for sound and would listen in on his telephone calls, played the role of a harmless and loyal civil servant to the hilt. He assumed an air of good-natured understanding, the attitude of a Cambridge gentleman who knew his friends must go through the process of investigating him regardless of his innocence.

In December 1951, Philby found himself called to MI5 headquarters at Leconfield House, a summons couched as a mild-mannered and courteous invitation. However, when he arrived, he found one of England's most ferocious prosecuting attorneys, Helenus "Buster" Milmo awaiting him. Milmo went on the attack, quizzing Philby relentlessly about the disappearance of Volkov, for the first time bringing up the massive spikes in radio traffic between London and Moscow, then Moscow and Istanbul, immediately following Philby's assignment to the case.

He went on to hammer Philby about Litzi's Comintern membership, about the Venona messages indicating that a young journalist matching Philby's career closely had been considered for a Soviet assassination attempt on Franco, about the deaths of hundreds of Albanians and Georgians due to the eerily precise foreknowledge the Soviets seemed to possess about the operations in practically every instance.

Philby parried every accusation smoothly, in a number of cases simply stating that he knew nothing and therefore could not answer. Milmo bellowed at Philby for four hours, exhausting both men, while Richard White, Guy Liddell, and other important MI5 men listened from the next room. Stewart Menzies of MI6 also listened in.

All of the men – Philby, Milmo, White, Liddell, and Menzies – knew that Philby worked as a Soviet agent by the end of the session. Philby knew that his former colleagues understood his betrayal in full, and they all acknowledged in their own writings that his reactions did not match outraged innocence. Instead, he displayed the calm slipperiness of an enemy agent who knew his adversaries' hands remained tied by the law absent overwhelming direct evidence (which they lacked) or a confession. Milmo wrote, "I find myself unable to avoid the conclusion that Philby is and has been for many years a Soviet agent [...] There's no hope of a confession, but he's as guilty as hell." (MacIntyre, 2015, 171).

The others concurred. With the failure of Milmo's bullying, they turned to the extremely cunning and persuasive William Skardon. Skardon had wheedled a confession out of Klaus Fuchs, but Philby proved beyond Skardon's power to crack. Despite multiple visits to Philby, Skardon got no further than Milmo.

Philby spent the next several years living in England for the most part, other than a brief trip to Spain looking for journalistic work. Aileen knew him to be a traitor, and her mental illness returned, prompting her to call the police and say that Philby had fled to Russia (he had not), drive her car into a storefront, and otherwise behave erratically. This won Philby some additional sympathy at MI6, particularly with Elliott, and Aileen's objectively deranged fantasies of Philby's flight when he continued living with her and their five children cast some doubt on the accusations themselves.

Philby finally found work at an import-export company. In the meantime, Anthony Blunt effectively gave up spying and engrossed himself in his passion, classical architecture. MI5 watched and waited for the opportunity to pounce, while Philby awaited their return with rather less anticipation.

Not until 1954 did the ghostly world of clandestine operations reach out to directly touch

Philby and the remaining members of the Cambridge Five again. In Canberra, Australia, the KGB colonel Vladimir Petrov decided to defect to the West on April 19th. A lurking KGB goon squad hustled Petrov's wife Evdokia aboard an aircraft, knocking one of her shoes off in the process.

Evdokia

Remarkably, a photograph of her seizure exists, showing two beefy KGB men, wearing baggy coats to conceal their weaponry, grasping her arms and marching her along, while her head is thrown back in distress, either over Petrov's defection or the fate possibly awaiting her in the Lubyanka. However, Australian Security Intelligence Organization (ASIO) men managed to rescue her when the aircraft touched down in Darwin to refuel, using the pretext that the carrying of weapons on flights represented a breach of law.

Philby soon got wind of Petrov's defection, responding with predictable alarm. Petrov confirmed that Burgess and Maclean remained alive and lived in Russia as defectors, the first certain news of the pair received by MI5 and MI6 since the their disappearance. Petrov also stated that a "Third Man" operated inside British intelligence, though he did not know the specific identity of this individual.

The Soviets realized that this news might panic Philby into rash action. He might turn himself in to the authorities, or attempt to flee abroad, in either case eliminating his future use as an intelligence asset. He might also betray Soviet operatives still in Britain in order to save his own skin. Accordingly, the KGB ordered Yuri Modin to make contact with Philby and provide him with a considerable sum of money in order to reassure him and keep him in the communist fold.

Modin accordingly prepared a bag of £5,000 cash (equivalent to £128,000 in 2018 money) from the KGB funds available to him. The problem remained of how to make contact with Philby given incessant MI5 surveillance.

Modin decided to make contact through Anthony Blunt. At first, Blunt ignored the prearranged signals for a meeting which Modin left near his apartment, probably not wishing to endanger his career as an art and architecture historian. Modin accordingly went to one of Blunt's lectures as a Norwegian with the name of Greenglass, carrying a postcard on the back of which he wrote "Tomorrow, 8 p.m., Ruislip," indicating that Blunt should meet him the following evening at Ruislip station. After the lecture, Modin waited for his opportunity to speak to Blunt amid his crowd of admirers: "Three young women, more zealous than the rest, blocked all the approaches to him […] I battered my way purposefully through his admirers, postcard in hand, elbowing one of the women hard in the ribs as I did so. 'Excuse me,' I grunted. 'Do you know where I can find this picture in the museum?' Blunt took the card, looked at it closely and gave me a long stare. 'Yes, yes, yes,' he said, answering all three of my written instructions with commendable brevity (Modin, 1994, 231).

Blunt arranged a meeting with Philby. Modin refused to meet with Philby directly, fearing to incriminate him, but did see him at a distance in a nighttime park as Blunt acted as a go-between, bringing the £5,000 to Philby along with Moscow's assurances of support. Both proved welcome. Philby, though living modestly, seriously lacked funds due to the interference of the suspicion against him with his ability to earn.

In October 1955, the newspapers printed accusations that Philby was the Third Man identified by Petrov. Philby met these accusations head-on, calling a major press conference and brazenly denying every charge against him. He also called on his accusers to present evidence, declaring with predatory cheerfulness that if they did not, he would be happy to sue them for libel if they repeated their assertions.

At this point, Nicolas Elliott, who remained loyal to his friend and refused to believe any of the accusations against him, exerted his influence at MI6 on Philby's behalf. With a new head of MI6 in place, and the bureau's tendency to defend its man against the accusations of the rival MI5, it did not prove difficult to secure Philby's return to MI6 service in 1956.

This time, MI6 made Philby an intelligence agent in Beirut. He would also work as a reporter for two magazines, the *Economist* and the *Observer*, providing him with an income of £3,000 and a cover for his activities. Journalism suited Philby well in any case. He would also work for the Beirut MI6 station, headed by Godfrey Paulson. This assignment, which gave Philby the chance to work his way back into MI6's good graces, effectively ended the Soviet agent's relationship with Aileen and his children, though he continued to pay their bills out of his now solid combined salary.

Lebanon now represented the same type of sordid, colorful, garish, dangerous, and varied scene, riddled with espionage, as had Istanbul during World War II. Philby settled into this venue as though into his native environment, and soon began providing "scoops" to both his overt and covert employers. He also took up with a tall, alcoholic, and married American woman, Eleanor Brewer.

A new KGB contact, Petukhov, soon approached Philby. The Englishman, rather than rejecting the overtures of his Soviet employers, immediately returned to the fold. At this point, he seemed addicted to intrigue and deception for its own sake – the excitement of playing many sides and navigating the hazardous maze between them. Aileen eventually died from alcoholism and a host of other ailments, many of them self-inflicted. Eleanor Brewer divorced her husband, who, despite knowing Philby had cuckolded him spectacularly, remained friendly to the English agent. In 1959, a year after Aileen's death, Philby married Eleanor Brewer.

Philby entered a phase of semi-retirement in which he did the minimum amount of journalism and spying needed to keep each of his jobs. This ended, however, when MI6 posted Philby's benefactor, Nicolas Elliott, to Beirut as well. Elliott's presence energized Philby again and he traveled widely and rapidly over the Middle East, sending an endless flurry of reports to MI6 through Elliott, as well as to the KGB.

In summer of 1960, Philby's father, St John Philby, then 65, stopped off in Beirut to visit his son. Elliott and Philby threw a munificent party for the elder Philby, at which father and son enjoyed each others' company for perhaps the first time in their lives. Bizarrely, St John Philby then went home, took a nap, went out to a nightclub the same night, and suffered a massive heart attack, uttering the words "God, I'm bored" as he died.

The death devastated Philby, who went on an immense drinking binge through the seediest taverns of Beirut for nearly a week afterward. Once he sobered up, Philby seemed to have lost his drive and spark.

Matters came to a head for Philby in late 1962 and early 1963. In 1962, MI6 uncovered the treason of an American in their service, George Blake, thanks to the information provided by a Polish defector, Michael Goleniewski. Blake, who had betrayed over 400 agents to the KGB, received a sentence of 42 years in prison, though he escaped his cell in 1966 and managed to reach the USSR.

Following this, Anatoly Golitsyn defected, revealing that Burgess and Maclean represented part of a "Ring of Five" men, mostly from Cambridge, who spied for the KGB. Though he did not know the names of the other three men in the "Ring," suspicion immediately fell upon Philby again. At this point, a friend of Philby's from long ago, Flora Solomon, approached MI5 and revealed that in the 1930s, Philby attempted to recruit her as a communist spy for Comintern. Though dubious – quite possibly correctly – about Solomon's own role in communist spying,

MI5 pounced on this piece of information, which provided independent corroboration of Philby's treason.

The new head of MI6, Richard White, confronted Nicolas Elliott with the new proof of Philby's Soviet ties. The proof simultaneously convinced, enraged, and devastated Elliott. All of their decades of friendship had concealed Philby's true purpose of making a dupe and tool of Elliott. Elliott expressed a desire to "shoot" Philby himself. Instead, Richard White sent the fuming MI6 on a mission to Lebanon, to confront Philby and force him to give up all his information to British intelligence.

Elliott took up residence in Beirut unobtrusively on January 10th, 1963. He then summoned Philby to hotel room. Philby instantly knew that he was finished, or, as he put it later, "the balloon was up." Depressed and broken, he nevertheless appeared, still swathed in bandages due to head injuries from a severe, drunken fall on New Year's. Elliott recorded their conversation, which proved to be very British and correct, but which clearly laid out that MI5 and MI6 now knew everything, and only a confession could save Philby. Only once during the interview did Elliott reveal his true fury, bellowing: "You took me in for years. Now I'll get the truth out of you even if I have to drag it out. You had to choose between Marxism and your family, and you chose Marxism. I once looked up to you, Kim. My God, how I despise you now. I hope you've enough decency left to understand why." (MacIntyre, 2015, 259).

Elliott offered two alternatives. Philby could either provide full details of his spy work, every KGB contact and operative he knew of, and every British agent working for the Soviets, in which case MI5 and MI6 would sweep the matter under the rug, allowing Philby to continue to live at the margins of society with enough money to keep him modestly provided for. Alternately, he could refuse, and British Intelligence would destroy him, ensuring he never worked again and died a pauper.

Elliott told Philby that new evidence had emerged against him. Philby did not even ask about the nature of this evidence. Instead, he left the first interview in silence, effectively providing a full admission of his guilt.

Over the next three days, Elliott and Philby met repeatedly. Philby provided a partial confession on the second day, typewritten and signed, in which he gave up only agents he knew to be either dead or already in the Soviet Union. However, this confession gave Elliott even more leverage over Philby; he could now be tried for treason if he failed to cooperate. Philby, however, continued to dodge, providing only partial information and a highly abbreviated version of his activities.

After the four day period of interrogation, Elliott flew on to the Congo, handing Philby's case over to Peter Lunn. Elliott left Philby unobserved for a day or two prior to Lunn's arrival, during which time Philby contacted Petukhov, telling him that MI5 had evidence against him but that he had confessed nothing. Moscow authorized Philby's extraction, but Petukhov could not arrange the English agent's escape immediately.

Lunn, however, proved no better at watching Philby than Elliott. In fact, the British allowed Philby so much freedom of action that it seems almost certain they had decided to allow him to slip away to the USSR. This would, hopefully, minimize the scandal, whereas a public trial or even confession would create a furor and massive demoralization in the country. It would also finish Philby as a Soviet agent as effectively as killing him would, without risking a diplomatic incident with the USSR.

Lunn said he would go skiing, though in fact he remained covertly in the city. On January 23rd, 1963, Philby saw Petukhov walk past on the street, reading a book – the prearranged signal that the Soviets had fully prepared his escape route. Accordingly, Philby told his wife he would be home for dinner and went out into a furious rainstorm then lashing Beirut.

Instead of returning home, however, Philby met Petukhov. KGB men drove him to the docks, where he took the place of Villi Maris, a Latvian sailor, on the Soviet freighter *Dolmatova*. A convivial KGB man, simultaneously, went out drinking with the real Maris, continuing until the Latvian fell unconscious. The ship sailed before morning, abandoning a portion of its cargo on the docks.

Eleanor contacted Peter Lunn in alarm when her husband did not return. Lunn, who had not gone on his alleged skiing trip, soon turned up at the Philby apartment. He reassured Eleanor as best as he could, telling her that Philby would turn up. He also appeared calm and unsurprised, lending more weight to the idea that the British allowed Philby to flee to simultaneously remove him permanently from anywhere that he could do them further harm and to avoid scandal.

Philby made an extremely impractical but good-faith effort to arrange for Eleanor to follow him by traveling to London, then booking a flight to Prague. Predictably, Philby's disappearance did not prevent a massive eruption of rage and recrimination between MI5, MI6, the FBI, and the CIA, but instead triggered it. The media seized on the story of the "Third Man," and the Soviets themselves gloated indirectly at their success by printing the newspaper headline, "Hello, Mr. Philby."

The Soviets treated Philby with a mixture of care for services rendered and contempt. They imported his favorite furniture, provided him with money, and also provided for his children in Britain with secret cash payments.

The defection of Philby effectively put an end to the active period of the Cambridge Five's service to the Soviets. He represented the most effective and highly placed of the five, and furnished the most damaging information to Britain's enemies, causing the deaths of thousands of anti-communist spies, agents, operatives, and partisans. The others had also played a role, but with his defection, other men took over the main levers of espionage.

Guy Burgess died of acute alcoholism in the same year that Philby came to the USSR, 1963, though Philby refused to see him before his death. Philby eventually married a much younger Russian woman, Rufina Ivanovna, and spent his later years lecturing young KGB recruits on the correct methods of spying, before his death in 1988.

Donald Maclean worked as a writer in the Soviet Union until his own death from pneumonia in 1983. John Cairncross confessed after Philby's flight and betrayed Anthony Blunt to his MI5 inquisitors. Both men made full confessions in exchange for immunity from prosecution and the British government's silence, though the media eventually learned that they represented the other two members of the Cambridge Five, bringing them full into the spotlight of international news.

Cairncross worked as a researcher of agricultural and petroleum topics for both the United Nations and various Italian investment banks. Blunt worked as an academic in the fields of art and architecture until his exposure, after which he went into seclusion for the remaining three years of his life until his death at age 75 in 1983.

While James Jesus Angleton, the American agent who had trusted in Philby, let the Englishman's betrayal haunt and destroy him, Nicolas Elliott refused to succumb to the shame of being turned into a dupe by his former friend. He remained a cheerful and active member of clubs, bought a racehorse, and entertained his friends with colorful anecdotes and risque stories. Eventually, he served as an intelligence adviser to Margaret Thatcher.

When Philby wrote a letter to Elliott on his own initiative, cheekily invoking their friendship and seeking to learn if he had escaped on his own or if the British had allowed him to flee Beirut. Elliott returned a one-line letter to his quondam comrade: "Put some flowers for me on poor Volkov's grave."

Online Resources

Other World War II titles by Charles River Editors

Other titles about World War II on Amazon

Other titles about the Cambridge Five on Amazon

Bibliography

Andrew, Christopher M. *The Defense of the Realm: The Authorized History of MI5.* London, 2009.

Borovik, Genrikh. *The Philby Files: The Secret Life of the Master Spy – KGB Archives*

Revealed. New York, 1995.

Costello, John, and Oleg Tsarev. *Deadly Illusions.* London, 1993.

Davies, Norman. *White Eagle, Red Star: The Polish-Soviet War 1919-1920 and the "Miracle on the Vistula."* London, 2003.

Hamrick, S.J. *Deceiving the Deceivers.* New Haven, 2004.

Holzman, Michael Howard. *James Jesus Angleton, the CIA, and the Craft of Counterintelligence.* Amherst, 2008.

Lownie, Andrew. *Stalin's Englishman: Guy Burgess, the Cold War, and the Cambridge Spy Ring.* New York, 2015.

MacIntyre, Ben. *A Spy Among Friends: Kim Philby and the Great Betrayal.* London, 2015.

Modin, Yuri, and Jean-Charles Deniau. *My Five Cambridge Friends.* New York, 1994.

Philby, Kim. *My Silent War: The Autobiography of Kim Philby.* London, 2003.

Free Books by Charles River Editors

We have brand new titles available for free most days of the week. To see which of our titles are currently free, click on this link.

Discounted Books by Charles River Editors

We have titles at a discount price of just 99 cents everyday. To see which of our titles are currently 99 cents, click on this link.

Printed in Great Britain
by Amazon